2022-2023
Monthly Planner

THIS BOOK BELONGS TO:

_____

Personal Information

Name: _____

Address: _____

City: _____ State: _____

Phone: _____

Email: _____

Emergency Contacts

Name: _____   Name: _____

Relationship: _____   Relationship: _____

Phone: _____   Phone: _____

Email: _____   Email: _____

Doctor: _____   Doctor: _____

Phone: _____   Phone: _____

Email: _____   Email: _____

Other

_____

_____

_____

_____

Contacts

Name: _____ Name: _____

Address: _____ Address: _____

Phone: _____ Phone: _____

Email: _____ Email: _____

Name: _____ Name: _____

Address: _____ Address: _____

Phone: _____ Phone: _____

Email: _____ Email: _____

Name: _____ Name: _____

Address: _____ Address: _____

Phone: _____ Phone: _____

Email: _____ Email: _____

Name: _____ Name: _____

Address: _____ Address: _____

Phone: _____ Phone: _____

Email: _____ Email: _____

Contacts

Name: _____ Name: _____

Address: _____ Address: _____

Phone: _____ Phone: _____

Email: _____ Email: _____

Name: _____ Name: _____

Address: _____ Address: _____

Phone: _____ Phone: _____

Email: _____ Email: _____

Name: _____ Name: _____

Address: _____ Address: _____

Phone: _____ Phone: _____

Email: _____ Email: _____

Name: _____ Name: _____

Address: _____ Address: _____

Phone: _____ Phone: _____

Email: _____ Email: _____

Password Log

Website:

Username:_____
Password:_____
Email Linked:_____
Membership Expiration Date:_____
Notes:_____

Website:

Username:_____
Password:_____
Email Linked:_____
Membership Expiration Date:_____
Notes:_____

Website:

Username:_____
Password:_____
Email Linked:_____
Membership Expiration Date:_____
Notes:_____

Website:

Username:_____
Password:_____
Email Linked:_____
Membership Expiration Date:_____
Notes:_____

Website:

Username:_____
Password:_____
Email Linked:_____
Membership Expiration Date:_____
Notes:_____

Website:

Username:_____
Password:_____
Email Linked:_____
Membership Expiration Date:_____
Notes:_____

Website:

Username:_____
Password:_____
Email Linked:_____
Membership Expiration Date:_____
Notes:_____

Website:

Username:_____
Password:_____
Email Linked:_____
Membership Expiration Date:_____
Notes:_____

Password Log

Website: _____

Username: _____

Password: _____

Email Linked: _____

Membership Expiration Date: _____

Notes: _____

Website: _____

Username: _____

Password: _____

Email Linked: _____

Membership Expiration Date: _____

Notes: _____

Website: _____

Username: _____

Password: _____

Email Linked: _____

Membership Expiration Date: _____

Notes: _____

Website: _____

Username: _____

Password: _____

Email Linked: _____

Membership Expiration Date: _____

Notes: _____

Website: _____

Username: _____

Password: _____

Email Linked: _____

Membership Expiration Date: _____

Notes: _____

Website: _____

Username: _____

Password: _____

Email Linked: _____

Membership Expiration Date: _____

Notes: _____

Website: _____

Username: _____

Password: _____

Email Linked: _____

Membership Expiration Date: _____

Notes: _____

Website: _____

Username: _____

Password: _____

Email Linked: _____

Membership Expiration Date: _____

Notes: _____

2022

January

Su	Mo	Tu	We	Th	Fr	Sa
						1
2	3	4	5	6	7	8
9	10	11	12	13	14	15
16	17	18	19	20	21	22
23	24	25	26	27	28	29
30	31					

February

Su	Mo	Tu	We	Th	Fr	Sa
		1	2	3	4	5
6	7	8	9	10	11	12
13	14	15	16	17	18	19
20	21	22	23	24	25	26
27	28					

March

Su	Mo	Tu	We	Th	Fr	Sa
		1	2	3	4	5
6	7	8	9	10	11	12
13	14	15	16	17	18	19
20	21	22	23	24	25	26
27	28	29	30	31		

April

Su	Mo	Tu	We	Th	Fr	Sa
					1	2
3	4	5	6	7	8	9
10	11	12	13	14	15	16
17	18	19	20	21	22	23
24	25	26	27	28	29	30

May

Su	Mo	Tu	We	Th	Fr	Sa
1	2	3	4	5	6	7
8	9	10	11	12	13	14
15	16	17	18	19	20	21
22	23	24	25	26	27	28
29	30	31				

June

Su	Mo	Tu	We	Th	Fr	Sa
			1	2	3	4
5	6	7	8	9	10	11
12	13	14	15	16	17	18
19	20	21	22	23	24	25
26	27	28	29	30		

July

Su	Mo	Tu	We	Th	Fr	Sa
					1	2
3	4	5	6	7	8	9
10	11	12	13	14	15	16
17	18	19	20	21	22	23
24	25	26	27	28	29	30
31						

August

Su	Mo	Tu	We	Th	Fr	Sa
	1	2	3	4	5	6
7	8	9	10	11	12	13
14	15	16	17	18	19	20
21	22	23	24	25	26	27
28	29	30	31			

September

Su	Mo	Tu	We	Th	Fr	Sa
				1	2	3
4	5	6	7	8	9	10
11	12	13	14	15	16	17
18	19	20	21	22	23	24
25	26	27	28	29	30	

October

Su	Mo	Tu	We	Th	Fr	Sa
						1
2	3	4	5	6	7	8
9	10	11	12	13	14	15
16	17	18	19	20	21	22
23	24	25	26	27	28	29
30	31					

November

Su	Mo	Tu	We	Th	Fr	Sa
		1	2	3	4	5
6	7	8	9	10	11	12
13	14	15	16	17	18	19
20	21	22	23	24	25	26
27	28	29	30			

December

Su	Mo	Tu	We	Th	Fr	Sa
				1	2	3
4	5	6	7	8	9	10
11	12	13	14	15	16	17
18	19	20	21	22	23	24
25	26	27	28	29	30	31

U.S. Holidays & Celebrations

Date	Day	Holiday	Notes
January 1, 2022	Saturday	New Year's Day	
January 17, 2022	Monday	Martin Luther King Jr. Day	
February 14, 2022	Monday	Valentine's Day	
February 21, 2022	Monday	President's Day	
April 17, 2022	Sunday	Easter Sunday	
April 18, 2022	Monday	Tax Day	
May 8, 2022	Sunday	Mother's Day	
May 30, 2022	Monday	Memorial Day	
June 19, 2022	Sunday	Father's Day	
July 4, 2022	Monday	Independence Day	
September 5, 2022	Monday	Labor Day	
October 10, 2022	Monday	Columbus Day	
October 31, 2022	Monday	Halloween	
November 11, 2022	Friday	Veterans Day	
November 24, 2022	Thursday	Thanksgiving Day	
November 25, 2022	Friday	Black Friday	
December 24, 2022	Saturday	Christmas Eve	
December 25, 2022	Sunday	Christmas Day	
December 26, 2022	Monday	Christmas Day (substitute day)	
December 31, 2022	Saturday	New Year's Eve	

Important Dates

January	February	March

April	May	June

July	August	September

October	November	December

Notes

January

Sunday	Monday	Tuesday	Wednesday
2	3	4	5
9	10	11	12
16	17 Martin Luther King Jr. Day	18	19
23	24	25	26
30	31		

December 2021

M	Tu	W	Th	F	Sa	Su
		1	2	3	4	5
6	7	8	9	10	11	12
13	14	15	16	17	18	19
20	21	22	23	24	25	26
27	28	29	30	31		

February 2022

M	Tu	W	Th	F	Sa	Su
	1	2	3	4	5	6
7	8	9	10	11	12	13
14	15	16	17	18	19	20
21	22	23	24	25	26	27
28						

2022

Thursday	Friday	Saturday
		1 New Year's Day
6	7 Orthodox Christmas	8
13	14	15
20	21	22
27	28	29

This Month's Focus

To-Do list

- ☐ _____
- ☐ _____
- ☐ _____
- ☐ _____
- ☐ _____
- ☐ _____
- ☐ _____
- ☐ _____
- ☐ _____
- ☐ _____
- ☐ _____
- ☐ _____

Notes

_____
_____
_____
_____
_____
_____
_____
_____
_____
_____
_____

Notes

Notes

February

Sunday	Monday	Tuesday	Wednesday
		1	2
6	7	8	9
13	14 Valentine's Day	15	16
20	21 President's Day	22	23
27	28		

January

M	Tu	W	Th	F	Sa	Su
					1	2
3	4	5	6	7	8	9
10	11	12	13	14	15	16
17	18	19	20	21	22	23
24	25	26	27	28	29	30
31						

March

M	Tu	W	Th	F	Sa	Su
	1	2	3	4	5	6
7	8	9	10	11	12	13
14	15	16	17	18	19	20
21	22	23	24	25	26	27
28	29	30	31			

2022

Thursday	Friday	Saturday
3	4	5
10	11	12
17	18	19
24	25	26

This Month's Focus

To-Do list

☐ _____
☐ _____
☐ _____
☐ _____
☐ _____
☐ _____
☐ _____
☐ _____
☐ _____
☐ _____
☐ _____
☐ _____

Notes

_____
_____
_____
_____
_____
_____
_____
_____
_____
_____

Notes

Notes

March

Sunday	Monday	Tuesday	Wednesday
		1	2 Ash Wednesday
6	7	8	9
13	14	15	16
20	21	22	23
27	28	29	30

February

M	Tu	W	Th	F	Sa	Su
	1	2	3	4	5	6
7	8	9	10	11	12	13
14	15	16	17	18	19	20
21	22	23	24	25	26	27
28						

April

M	Tu	W	Th	F	Sa	Su
				1	2	3
4	5	6	7	8	9	10
11	12	13	14	15	16	17
18	19	20	21	22	23	24
25	26	27	28	29	30	

2022

Thursday	Friday	Saturday
3	4	5
10	11	12
17 St Patricks Day	18	19
24	25	26
31		

This Month's Focus

To-Do list

- ☐ _____
- ☐ _____
- ☐ _____
- ☐ _____
- ☐ _____
- ☐ _____
- ☐ _____
- ☐ _____
- ☐ _____
- ☐ _____
- ☐ _____
- ☐ _____

Notes

_____
_____
_____
_____
_____
_____
_____
_____
_____
_____
_____

Notes

Notes

April

Sunday	Monday	Tuesday	Wednesday
3	4	5	6
10 Palm Sunday	11	12	13
17 Easter Sunday	18 Tax Day	19	20
24 Orthodox Easter	25	26	27

March

M	Tu	W	Th	F	Sa	Su
	1	2	3	4	5	6
7	8	9	10	11	12	13
14	15	16	17	18	19	20
21	22	23	24	25	26	27
28	29	30	31			

May

M	Tu	W	Th	F	Sa	Su
						1
2	3	4	5	6	7	8
9	10	11	12	13	14	15
16	17	18	19	20	21	22
23	24	25	26	27	28	29
31						

2022

Thursday	Friday	Saturday
	1	2
7	8	9
14	15 Good Friday	16
21	22	23
28	29	30

This Month's Focus

To-Do list

- ☐ _____
- ☐ _____
- ☐ _____
- ☐ _____
- ☐ _____
- ☐ _____
- ☐ _____
- ☐ _____
- ☐ _____
- ☐ _____
- ☐ _____
- ☐ _____

Notes

_____
_____
_____
_____
_____
_____
_____
_____
_____
_____
_____
_____

Notes

Notes

May

Sunday	Monday	Tuesday	Wednesday
1	2	3	4
8 Mother's Day	9	10	11
15	16	17	18
22	23	24	25
29	30 Memorial Day	31	

April

M	Tu	W	Th	F	Sa	Su
				1	2	3
4	5	6	7	8	9	10
11	12	13	14	15	16	17
18	19	20	21	22	23	24
25	26	27	28	29	30	

June

M	Tu	W	Th	F	Sa	Su
		1	2	3	4	5
6	7	8	9	10	11	12
13	14	15	16	17	18	19
20	21	22	23	24	25	26
27	28	29	30			

2022

Thursday	Friday	Saturday
5	6	7
12	13	14
19	20	21
26	27	28

This Month's Focus

To-Do list

☐ _____
☐ _____
☐ _____
☐ _____
☐ _____
☐ _____
☐ _____
☐ _____
☐ _____
☐ _____
☐ _____
☐ _____

Notes

_____
_____
_____
_____
_____
_____
_____
_____
_____
_____

Notes

Notes

June

Sunday	Monday	Tuesday	Wednesday
			1
5	6	7	8
12	13	14	15
19 Juneteenth Father's Day	20 Juneteenth (Observed)	21	22
26	27	28	29

May

M	Tu	W	Th	F	Sa	Su
						1
2	3	4	5	6	7	8
9	10	11	12	13	14	15
16	17	18	19	20	21	22
23	24	25	26	27	28	29
31						

July

M	Tu	W	Th	F	Sa	Su
				1	2	3
4	5	6	7	8	9	10
11	12	13	14	15	16	17
18	19	20	21	22	23	24
25	26	27	28	29	30	31

2022

Thursday	Friday	Saturday
2	3	4
9	10	11
16	17	18
23	24	25
30		

This Month's Focus

To-Do list

☐ _____
☐ _____
☐ _____
☐ _____
☐ _____
☐ _____
☐ _____
☐ _____
☐ _____
☐ _____
☐ _____
☐ _____

Notes

_____
_____
_____
_____
_____
_____
_____
_____
_____
_____
_____

Notes

Notes

July

Sunday	Monday	Tuesday	Wednesday
3	4 Independence Day	5	6
10	11	12	13
17	18	19	20
24	25	26	27
31			

June

M	Tu	W	Th	F	Sa	Su
		1	2	3	4	5
6	7	8	9	10	11	12
13	14	15	16	17	18	19
20	21	22	23	24	25	26
27	28	29	30			

August

M	Tu	W	Th	F	Sa	Su
1	2	3	4	5	6	7
8	9	10	11	12	13	14
15	16	17	18	19	20	21
22	23	24	25	26	27	28
29	30	31				

2022

Thursday	Friday	Saturday
	1	2
7	8	9
14	15	16
21	22	23
28	29	30

This Month's Focus

To-Do list

- ☐ _____
- ☐ _____
- ☐ _____
- ☐ _____
- ☐ _____
- ☐ _____
- ☐ _____
- ☐ _____
- ☐ _____
- ☐ _____
- ☐ _____
- ☐ _____

Notes

_____
_____
_____
_____
_____
_____
_____
_____
_____
_____

Notes

Notes

August

Sunday	Monday	Tuesday	Wednesday
	1	2	3
7	8	9	10
14	15	16	17
21	22	23	24
28	29	30	31

		July	September

July

M	Tu	W	Th	F	Sa	Su
				1	2	3
4	5	6	7	8	9	10
11	12	13	14	15	16	17
18	19	20	21	22	23	24
25	26	27	28	29	30	31

September

M	Tu	W	Th	F	Sa	Su
			1	2	3	4
5	6	7	8	9	10	11
12	13	14	15	16	17	18
19	20	21	22	23	24	25
26	27	28	29	30		

2022

Thursday	Friday	Saturday
4	5	6
11	12	13
18	19	20
25	26	27

This Month's Focus

To-Do list

- ☐ _____
- ☐ _____
- ☐ _____
- ☐ _____
- ☐ _____
- ☐ _____
- ☐ _____
- ☐ _____
- ☐ _____
- ☐ _____
- ☐ _____
- ☐ _____

Notes

_____
_____
_____
_____
_____
_____
_____
_____
_____
_____
_____

Notes

Notes

September

Sunday	Monday	Tuesday	Wednesday
4	5 Labor Day	6	7
11	12	13	14
18	19	20	21
25	26 Rosh Hashanah	27	28

August

M	Tu	W	Th	F	Sa	Su
1	2	3	4	5	6	7
8	9	10	11	12	13	14
15	16	17	18	19	20	21
22	23	24	25	26	27	28
29	30	31				

October

M	Tu	W	Th	F	Sa	Su
					1	2
3	4	5	6	7	8	9
10	11	12	13	14	15	16
17	18	19	20	21	22	23
24	25	26	27	28	29	30
31						

2022

Thursday	Friday	Saturday
1	2	3
8	9	10
15	16	17
22	23	24
29	30	

This Month's Focus

To-Do list

- ☐ _____
- ☐ _____
- ☐ _____
- ☐ _____
- ☐ _____
- ☐ _____
- ☐ _____
- ☐ _____
- ☐ _____
- ☐ _____
- ☐ _____
- ☐ _____

Notes

_____
_____
_____
_____
_____
_____
_____
_____
_____
_____
_____

Notes

Notes

October

Sunday	Monday	Tuesday	Wednesday
2	3	4	5 Yom Kippur
9	10 Columbus Day	11	12
16	17	18	19
23	24	25	26
30	31 Halloween		

September

M	Tu	W	Th	F	Sa	Su
				1	2	3	4
5	6	7	8	9	10	11
12	13	14	15	16	17	18
19	20	21	22	23	24	25
26	27	28	29	30		

November

M	Tu	W	Th	F	Sa	Su
	1	2	3	4	5	6
7	8	9	10	11	12	13
14	15	16	17	18	19	20
21	22	23	24	25	26	27
28	29	30				

2022

Thursday	Friday	Saturday
		1
6	7	8
13	14	15
20	21	22
27	28	29

This Month's Focus

To-Do list

- ☐ _____
- ☐ _____
- ☐ _____
- ☐ _____
- ☐ _____
- ☐ _____
- ☐ _____
- ☐ _____
- ☐ _____
- ☐ _____
- ☐ _____
- ☐ _____

Notes

_____
_____
_____
_____
_____
_____
_____
_____
_____
_____
_____

Notes

Notes

November

Sunday	Monday	Tuesday	Wednesday
		1	2
6	7	8	9
13	14	15	16
20	21	22	23
27	28	29	30
		October	December

October

M	Tu	W	Th	F	Sa	Su
					1	2
3	4	5	6	7	8	9
10	11	12	13	14	15	16
17	18	19	20	21	22	23
24	25	26	27	28	29	30
31						

December

M	Tu	W	Th	F	Sa	Su
			1	2	3	4
5	6	7	8	9	10	11
12	13	14	15	16	17	18
19	20	21	22	23	24	25
26	27	28	29	30	31	

2022

Thursday	Friday	Saturday
3	4	5
10	11 Veterans Day	12
17	18	19
24 Thanksgiving Day	25	26

This Month's Focus

To-Do list

☐ _____
☐ _____
☐ _____
☐ _____
☐ _____
☐ _____
☐ _____
☐ _____
☐ _____
☐ _____
☐ _____
☐ _____

Notes

_____
_____
_____
_____
_____
_____
_____
_____
_____
_____
_____

Notes

Notes

December

Sunday	Monday	Tuesday	Wednesday
4	5	6	7
11	12	13	14
18	19	20	21
25 Christmas Day	26 Christmas Day (Observed)	27	28

November 2022

M	Tu	W	Th	F	Sa	Su
	1	2	3	4	5	6
7	8	9	10	11	12	13
14	15	16	17	18	19	20
21	22	23	24	25	26	27
28	29	30				

January 2023

M	Tu	W	Th	F	Sa	Su
						1
2	3	4	5	6	7	8
9	10	11	12	13	14	15
16	17	18	19	20	21	22
23	24	25	26	27	28	29
30	31					

2022

Thursday	Friday	Saturday
1	2	3
8	9	10
15	16	17
22	23	24 Christmas Eve
29	30	31 New Year's Eve

This Month's Focus

To-Do list

☐ _____
☐ _____
☐ _____
☐ _____
☐ _____
☐ _____
☐ _____
☐ _____
☐ _____
☐ _____
☐ _____
☐ _____

Notes

_____
_____
_____
_____
_____
_____
_____
_____
_____
_____
_____

Notes

Notes

2023

January

Su	Mo	Tu	We	Th	Fr	Sa
1	2	3	4	5	6	7
8	9	10	11	12	13	14
15	16	17	18	19	20	21
22	23	24	25	26	27	28
29	30	31				

February

Su	Mo	Tu	We	Th	Fr	Sa
			1	2	3	4
5	6	7	8	9	10	11
12	13	14	15	16	17	18
19	20	21	22	23	24	25
26	27	28				

March

Su	Mo	Tu	We	Th	Fr	Sa
			1	2	3	4
5	6	7	8	9	10	11
12	13	14	15	16	17	18
19	20	21	22	23	24	25
26	27	28	29	30	31	

April

Su	Mo	Tu	We	Th	Fr	Sa
						1
2	3	4	5	6	7	8
9	10	11	12	13	14	15
16	17	18	19	20	21	22
23	24	25	26	27	28	29
30						

May

Su	Mo	Tu	We	Th	Fr	Sa
	1	2	3	4	5	6
7	8	9	10	11	12	13
14	15	16	17	18	19	20
21	22	23	24	25	26	27
28	29	30	31			

June

Su	Mo	Tu	We	Th	Fr	Sa
				1	2	3
4	5	6	7	8	9	10
11	12	13	14	15	16	17
18	19	20	21	22	23	24
25	26	27	28	29	30	

July

Su	Mo	Tu	We	Th	Fr	Sa
						1
2	3	4	5	6	7	8
9	10	11	12	13	14	15
16	17	18	19	20	21	22
23	24	25	26	27	28	29
30	31					

August

Su	Mo	Tu	We	Th	Fr	Sa
		1	2	3	4	5
6	7	8	9	10	11	12
13	14	15	16	17	18	19
20	21	22	23	24	25	26
27	28	29	30	31		

September

Su	Mo	Tu	We	Th	Fr	Sa
					1	2
3	4	5	6	7	8	9
10	11	12	13	14	15	16
17	18	19	20	21	22	23
24	25	26	27	28	29	30

October

Su	Mo	Tu	We	Th	Fr	Sa
1	2	3	4	5	6	7
8	9	10	11	12	13	14
15	16	17	18	19	20	21
22	23	24	25	26	27	28
29	30	31				

November

Su	Mo	Tu	We	Th	Fr	Sa
			1	2	3	4
5	6	7	8	9	10	11
12	13	14	15	16	17	18
19	20	21	22	23	24	25
26	27	28	29	30		

December

Su	Mo	Tu	We	Th	Fr	Sa
					1	2
3	4	5	6	7	8	9
10	11	12	13	14	15	16
17	18	19	20	21	22	23
24	25	26	27	28	29	30
31						

U.S. Holidays & Celebrations

Date	Day	Holiday	Notes
January 1, 2023	Sunday	New Year's Day	
January 16, 2023	Monday	Martin Luther King Jr. Day	
February 14, 2023	Tuesday	Valentine's Day	
February 20, 2023	Monday	President's Day	
April 9, 2023	Sunday	Easter Sunday	
April 18, 2023	Tuesday	Tax Day	
May 14, 2023	Sunday	Mother's Day	
May 29, 2023	Monday	Memorial Day	
June 18, 2023	Sunday	Father's Day	
July 4, 2023	Tuesday	Independence Day	
September 4, 2023	Monday	Labor Day	
October 9, 2023	Monday	Columbus Day	
October 31, 2023	Tuesday	Halloween	
November 11, 2023	Saturday	Veterans Day	
November 23, 2023	Thursday	Thanksgiving Day	
November 24, 2023	Friday	Black Friday	
December 24, 2023	Sunday	Christmas Eve	
December 25, 2023	Monday	Christmas Day	
December 26, 2023	Tuesday	Christmas Day (substitute day)	
December 31, 2023	Sunday	New Year's Eve	

Important Dates

January	February	March

April	May	June

July	August	September

October	November	December

Notes

January

Sunday	Monday	Tuesday	Wednesday
1 New Year's Day	2 New Year's Day (Observed)	3	4
8	9	10	11
15	16 Martin Luther King Jr. Day	17	18
22	23	24	25
29	30	31	

December 2022

M	Tu	W	Th	F	Sa	Su
			1	2	3	4
5	6	7	8	9	10	11
12	13	14	15	16	17	18
19	20	21	22	23	24	25
26	27	28	29	30	31	

February 2023

M	Tu	W	Th	F	Sa	Su
		1	2	3	4	5
6	7	8	9	10	11	12
13	14	15	16	17	18	19
20	21	22	23	24	25	26
27	28					

2023

Thursday	Friday	Saturday
5	6	7 Orthodox Christmas
12	13	14
19	20	21
26	27	28

This Month's Focus

To-Do list

☐ _____
☐ _____
☐ _____
☐ _____
☐ _____
☐ _____
☐ _____
☐ _____
☐ _____
☐ _____
☐ _____
☐ _____

Notes

_____
_____
_____
_____
_____
_____
_____
_____
_____
_____
_____

Notes

Notes

February

Sunday	Monday	Tuesday	Wednesday
			1
5	6	7	8
12	13	14 Valentine's Day	15
19	20 President's Day	21	22 Ash Wednesday
26	27	28	

January

M	Tu	W	Th	F	Sa	Su
						1
2	3	4	5	6	7	8
9	10	11	12	13	14	15
16	17	18	19	20	21	22
23	24	25	26	27	28	29
30	31					

March

M	Tu	W	Th	F	Sa	Su
		1	2	3	4	5
6	7	8	9	10	11	12
13	14	15	16	17	18	19
20	21	22	23	24	25	26
27	28	29	30	31		

2023

Thursday	Friday	Saturday
2	3	4
9	10	11
16	17	18
23	24	25

This Month's Focus

To-Do list

☐ _____
☐ _____
☐ _____
☐ _____
☐ _____
☐ _____
☐ _____
☐ _____
☐ _____
☐ _____
☐ _____
☐ _____

Notes

_____
_____
_____
_____
_____
_____
_____
_____
_____
_____

Notes

Notes

March

Sunday	Monday	Tuesday	Wednesday
			1
5	6	7	8
12	13	14	15
19	20	21	22
26	27	28	29

February

M	Tu	W	Th	F	Sa	Su
			1	2	3	4	5
6	7	8	9	10	11	12
13	14	15	16	17	18	19
20	21	22	23	24	25	26
27	28					

April

M	Tu	W	Th	F	Sa	Su
					1	2
3	4	5	6	7	8	9
10	11	12	13	14	15	16
17	18	19	20	21	22	23
24	25	26	27	28	29	30

2023

Thursday	Friday	Saturday
2	3	4
9	10	11
16	17 St Patricks Day	18
23	24	25
30	31	

This Month's Focus

To-Do list

☐ _____
☐ _____
☐ _____
☐ _____
☐ _____
☐ _____
☐ _____
☐ _____
☐ _____
☐ _____
☐ _____
☐ _____

Notes

Notes

Notes

April

Sunday	Monday	Tuesday	Wednesday
2 Palm Sunday	3	4	5
9 Easter Sunday	10	11	12
16 Orthodox Easter	17	18 Tax Day	19
23	24	25	26
30			

March

M	Tu	W	Th	F	Sa	Su
		1	2	3	4	5
6	7	8	9	10	11	12
13	14	15	16	17	18	19
20	21	22	23	24	25	26
27	28	29	30	31		

May

M	Tu	W	Th	F	Sa	Su
1	2	3	4	5	6	7
8	9	10	11	12	13	14
15	16	17	18	19	20	21
22	23	24	25	26	27	28
29	30	31				

2023

Thursday	Friday	Saturday
		1
6	7 Good Friday	8
13	14	15
20	21	22
27	28	29

This Month's Focus

To-Do list

- ☐ _____
- ☐ _____
- ☐ _____
- ☐ _____
- ☐ _____
- ☐ _____
- ☐ _____
- ☐ _____
- ☐ _____
- ☐ _____
- ☐ _____
- ☐ _____

Notes

_____
_____
_____
_____
_____
_____
_____
_____
_____
_____

Notes

Notes

May

Sunday	Monday	Tuesday	Wednesday
	1	2	3
7	8	9	10
14 Mother's Day	15	16	17
21	22	23	24
28	29 Memorial Day	30	31

April

M	Tu	W	Th	F	Sa	Su
					1	2
3	4	5	6	7	8	9
10	11	12	13	14	15	16
17	18	19	20	21	22	23
24	25	26	27	28	29	30

June

M	Tu	W	Th	F	Sa	Su
			1	2	3	4
5	6	7	8	9	10	11
12	13	14	15	16	17	18
19	20	21	22	23	24	25
26	27	28	29	30		

2023

Thursday	Friday	Saturday
4	5	6
11	12	13
18	19	20
25	26	27

This Month's Focus

To-Do list

☐ _____
☐ _____
☐ _____
☐ _____
☐ _____
☐ _____
☐ _____
☐ _____
☐ _____
☐ _____
☐ _____
☐ _____

Notes

_____
_____
_____
_____
_____
_____
_____
_____
_____
_____
_____

Notes

Notes

June

Sunday	Monday	Tuesday	Wednesday
4	5	6	7
11	12	13	14
18 Father's Day	19 Juneteenth	20	21
25	26	27	28

May

M	Tu	W	Th	F	Sa	Su
1	2	3	4	5	6	7
8	9	10	11	12	13	14
15	16	17	18	19	20	21
22	23	24	25	26	27	28
29	30	31				

July

M	Tu	W	Th	F	Sa	Su
					1	2
3	4	5	6	7	8	9
10	11	12	13	14	15	16
17	18	19	20	21	22	23
24	25	26	27	28	29	30
31						

2023

Thursday	Friday	Saturday
1	2	3
8	9	10
15	16	17
22	23	24
29	30	

This Month's Focus

To-Do list

☐ _____
☐ _____
☐ _____
☐ _____
☐ _____
☐ _____
☐ _____
☐ _____
☐ _____
☐ _____
☐ _____
☐ _____

Notes

_____
_____
_____
_____
_____
_____
_____
_____
_____
_____
_____

Notes

Notes

July

Sunday	Monday	Tuesday	Wednesday
2	3	4 Independence Day	5
9	10	11	12
16	17	18	19
23	24	25	26
30	31		

June

M	Tu	W	Th	F	Sa	Su
			1	2	3	4
5	6	7	8	9	10	11
12	13	14	15	16	17	18
19	20	21	22	23	24	25
26	27	28	29	30		

August

M	Tu	W	Th	F	Sa	Su
	1	2	3	4	5	6
7	8	9	10	11	12	13
14	15	16	17	18	19	20
21	22	23	24	25	26	27
28	29	30	31			

2023

Thursday	Friday	Saturday
		1
6	7	8
13	14	15
20	21	22
27	28	29

This Month's Focus

To-Do list

- ☐ _____
- ☐ _____
- ☐ _____
- ☐ _____
- ☐ _____
- ☐ _____
- ☐ _____
- ☐ _____
- ☐ _____
- ☐ _____
- ☐ _____
- ☐ _____

Notes

_____
_____
_____
_____
_____
_____
_____
_____
_____
_____

Notes

Notes

August

Sunday	Monday	Tuesday	Wednesday
		1	2
6	7	8	9
13	14	15	16
20	21	22	23
27	28	29	30

July

M	Tu	W	Th	F	Sa	Su
					1	2
3	4	5	6	7	8	9
10	11	12	13	14	15	16
17	18	19	20	21	22	23
24	25	26	27	28	29	30
31						

September

M	Tu	W	Th	F	Sa	Su
				1	2	3
4	5	6	7	8	9	10
11	12	13	14	15	16	17
18	19	20	21	22	23	24
25	26	27	28	29	30	

2023

Thursday	Friday	Saturday
3	4	5
10	11	12
17	18	19
24	25	26
31		

This Month's Focus

To-Do list

☐ _____
☐ _____
☐ _____
☐ _____
☐ _____
☐ _____
☐ _____
☐ _____
☐ _____
☐ _____
☐ _____
☐ _____

Notes

_____
_____
_____
_____
_____
_____
_____
_____
_____
_____

Notes

Notes

September

Sunday	Monday	Tuesday	Wednesday
3	4 Labor Day	5	6
10	11	12	13
17	18	19	20
24	25 Yom Kippur	26	27
		August M Tu W Th F Sa Su 1 2 3 4 5 6 7 8 9 10 11 12 13 14 15 16 17 18 19 20 21 22 23 24 25 26 27 28 29 30 31	**October** M Tu W Th F Sa Su 1 2 3 4 5 6 7 8 9 10 11 12 13 14 15 16 17 18 19 20 21 22 23 24 25 26 27 28 29 31

2023

Thursday	Friday	Saturday
	1	2
7	8	9
14	15	16 Rosh Hashanah
21	22	23
28	29	30

This Month's Focus

To-Do list

- ☐ _____
- ☐ _____
- ☐ _____
- ☐ _____
- ☐ _____
- ☐ _____
- ☐ _____
- ☐ _____
- ☐ _____
- ☐ _____
- ☐ _____
- ☐ _____

Notes

_____
_____
_____
_____
_____
_____
_____
_____
_____
_____

Notes

Notes

October

Sunday	Monday	Tuesday	Wednesday
1	2	3	4
8	9 Columbus Day	10	11
15	16	17	18
22	23	24	25
29	30	31 Halloween	

September

M	Tu	W	Th	F	Sa	Su
				1	2	3
4	5	6	7	8	9	10
11	12	13	14	15	16	17
18	19	20	21	22	23	24
25	26	27	28	29	30	

November

M	Tu	W	Th	F	Sa	Su
	1	2	3	4	5
6	7	8	9	10	11	12
13	14	15	16	17	18	19
20	21	22	23	24	25	26
27	28	29	30			

2023

Thursday	Friday	Saturday
5	6	7
12	13	14
19	20	21
26	27	28

This Month's Focus

To-Do list

☐ _____
☐ _____
☐ _____
☐ _____
☐ _____
☐ _____
☐ _____
☐ _____
☐ _____
☐ _____
☐ _____
☐ _____

Notes

_____
_____
_____
_____
_____
_____
_____
_____
_____
_____
_____

Notes

Notes

November

Sunday	Monday	Tuesday	Wednesday
			1
5	6	7	8
12	13	14	15
19	20	21	22
26	27	28	29

October

M	Tu	W	Th	F	Sa	Su
						1
2	3	4	5	6	7	8
9	10	11	12	13	14	15
16	17	18	19	20	21	22
23	24	25	26	27	28	29
31						

December

M	Tu	W	Th	F	Sa	Su
				1	2	3
4	5	6	7	8	9	10
11	12	13	14	15	16	17
18	19	20	21	22	23	24
25	26	27	28	29	30	31

2023

Thursday	Friday	Saturday
2	3	4
9	10 Veterans Day (Observed)	11 Veterans Day
16	17	18
23 Thanksgiving Day	24	25
30		

This Month's Focus

To-Do list

- ☐ _____
- ☐ _____
- ☐ _____
- ☐ _____
- ☐ _____
- ☐ _____
- ☐ _____
- ☐ _____
- ☐ _____
- ☐ _____
- ☐ _____
- ☐ _____

Notes

_____
_____
_____
_____
_____
_____
_____
_____
_____
_____

Notes

Notes

December

Sunday	Monday	Tuesday	Wednesday
3	4	5	6
10	11	12	13
17	18	19	20
24 Christmas Eve	25 Christmas Day	26	27
31 New Year's Eve			

November 2023

M	Tu	W	Th	F	Sa	Su
		1	2	3	4	5
6	7	8	9	10	11	12
13	14	15	16	17	18	19
20	21	22	23	24	25	26
27	28	29	30			

January 2024

M	Tu	W	Th	F	Sa	Su
1	2	3	4	5	6	7
8	9	10	11	12	13	14
15	16	17	18	19	20	21
22	23	24	25	26	27	28
29	30	31				

2023

Thursday	Friday	Saturday
	1	2
7	8	9
14	15	16
21	22	23
28	29	30

This Month's Focus

To-Do list

- ☐ _____
- ☐ _____
- ☐ _____
- ☐ _____
- ☐ _____
- ☐ _____
- ☐ _____
- ☐ _____
- ☐ _____
- ☐ _____
- ☐ _____
- ☐ _____

Notes

_____
_____
_____
_____
_____
_____
_____
_____
_____
_____

Notes

Notes

Thank you!

We'd like to know what you think!

Your opinion matters to us, please do not hesitate
to leave a comment on the Amazon website.

Made in the USA
Monee, IL
22 September 2021